# The Princess and the Baby

EXODUS 1:8 – 2:10 FOR CHILDREN

Written by Janice Kramer          Illustrated by Sally Mathews

RCH® Books

1969 CONCORDIA PUBLISHING HOUSE, ST. LOUIS, MISSOURI

ANUFACTURED IN THE UNITED STATES OF AMERICA
L RIGHTS RESERVED
N 0-570-06043-5

The wicked king of Egypt was
as worried as could be.
"Israelites!" he fumed and fussed.
"That's all I ever see!
They work our land.
They breathe our air.
Those Israelites are everywhere!
If I'm not careful, some fine day
they'll up and take my land away!

"I'll make them suffer. Then they'll leave,
and Egypt will be mine.
Those Israelites will know this king
is not without a spine!"
He made them carry stones and sticks
and great big heavy loads of bricks.
And worst of all, he planned to kill
the baby boys of Israel!

Oh, what a wicked man he was
to think of such a thing!
But many of the Israelites
were smarter than the king.
They hid their baby boys from sight
and kept them hidden day and night.
They prayed and prayed that God above
would help them with His strength and love.

One mother tried to keep her baby
quiet as a mouse.
But every day the soldiers
of the king rode by her house.
"If he should cry as they pass by,
they'll know he's here, and he will die.
My baby must be kept alive!
Somehow, someway he must survive!"

And so that loving mother made
a tiny little boat.
With loving care she made it strong
so it was sure to float.
She dressed her baby in his clothes,
then kissed him on his little nose
and tucked him in with blankets round
to keep him warm and safe and sound.

The baby's sister Miriam
was puzzled through and through.
"Why, Mother!" cried the little girl,
"What *are* you going to do?"
"You'll see," the mother said, "You'll see.
Be quiet now and follow me."
Then out the door with cautious eye
she looked for soldiers passing by.

The way was clear. She gathered up
her baby, boat and all.
"Stay right beside me, Miriam.
Be careful not to fall."
They walked together one long mile
until they reached the River Nile.
And then the little girl began
to understand her mother's plan.

And when they reached the river's edge,
they put the strong boat in,
then laid the baby down inside.
No water touched his skin.
He didn't cry or make a peep,
he simply yawned and went to sleep.
The mother wiped away a tear.
"The king will never find him here."

"Oh, Mother," said the little girl,
"I'll stay with him all day.
If anyone should come, I'll just
pretend I'm here to play."
The mother kissed her daughter's face
and held her in a long embrace.
"My little girl," she said with pride,
"has suddenly grown up inside!"

With that the mother hurried home;
she had been gone too long.
Now would the soldiers start to think
that something had gone wrong?
Poor Miriam was all alone.
She sat for hours on a stone
and watched the baby slumber on.
How strange it seemed with Mother gone!

Then suddenly she heard a sound
upon the river path.
"Three ladies!" whispered Miriam.
"They've come to take a bath!
Oh, no! The one that's chattering,
she is the daughter of the king.
He murders little baby boys.
I mustn't make a single noise!"

She ducked and hid, but all was lost —
they'd seen the little boat!
"Why, look!" the princess cried aloud.
"A little baby boy afloat!"
She picked him up, and how he cried!
"An Israelite," the princess sighed.
"But he's so sweet, as sweet can be.
I'll take him home to live with me!"

The ladies hadn't noticed
that young Miriam was there.
So she approached them now as if
she didn't have a care.
"Hello!" she said. "I'm almost nine.
And don't you think the weather's fine?
What have you there? Why, goodness me!
Is that a baby boy I see?"

"Why, yes, it is," the princess said.
"I found him floating over there."
"You'll need a nurse," said Miriam,
"to give him proper care.
I know a lady Israelite
who'd nurse him for you day and night."
The princess answered thankfully,
"Please go and bring her here to me."

When Miriam came back, she had
her mother by the hand!
Then bowing low, the mother said,
"I'll do what you command."
The princess looked at her and smiled.
"I'll pay you well to nurse this child.
Take care of him until he's grown,
and love him as your very own."